find me there

sara rian

Artwork by Anne Kostecki ©

ISBN 9798878469159

this book is dedicated to all those who pick it up
and see their grief and love in the pages.

find me there.
where sunsets glow
but it never gets dark.
where pain doesn't exist
and comfort is always felt.
where everything you've ever loved
finds its way back to you in the end.
the place you went to when
your heart fell asleep.
my time will come
to see you again
and you can
find me
there.

s a r a r i a n

find me there

sara rian

the wish
to be with you there
sits on one side of me.
the desire to make
you proud here
sits on the other.
and between them
i'll sway
until i have both.

find me there

sara rian

as your hand
slipped from mine
grief took the other
and promised to
never let go.

find me there

sara rian

a little card
with a little poem
and a little picture.
sitting in a little dish.
often too little to notice
in a room filled with grief.
until it was your face
on that little card.
now tucked in my purse.
and on my windshield.
the meaning that it holds.
proof that you really died.
the deep pain in my chest
when i glance its way.
as we often realize in grief
the little things aren't
so little anymore.

find me there

sara rian

two things died that day.
you.
and the chance
to ever feel whole again.

find me there

sara rian

i remember a girl at the funeral.
her eyes so lost and glazed over.
red. raw. pushed beyond their limit.
love and agony draining from her mind
and out of those eyes. hour after hour.
we took the same steps around the room.
we hugged the same people at the casket.
and it was not until i stood in the mirror
that i realized that girl was *me*.

and i will never forget
her eyes.

find me there

sara rian

they tell us to wear all black.

but i didn't listen.
black is the absence of light
and my world lost enough
of that when you died.
so i said goodbye
in red.

find me there

sara rian

nothing will be enough.
besides feeling their heart
beating next to mine again.
no amount of stories. songs.
pictures. dreams. or smells
can make anything better.
but i want them anyway.
in grief i am a beggar.
not a chooser.

find me there

sara rian

i lost you.
but not like how one
misplaces their keys.
you cannot just walk away
and forget to take your heart with you.
you were taken. pulled into another world.
i will still search for you everywhere
but i know i won't find you here.

find me there

sara rian

you slipped away and now
the sun comes out at night.
the moon, in the morning.
my summers are cold.
my winters feel hot.
sugar tastes bitter.
i cry when i smile.
and nothing
makes sense
without you.

find me there

sara rian

i just wanted it all.
to have had you
and to have kept you.
to be lucky enough to be yours
and to have had all the years together
that we were supposed to have.
i am tired of asking myself
if i'd trade everything i have now
to have you back here with me.
why i couldn't have both
i will never know
and may never accept.

find me there

sara rian

i don't want to be a fighter.
i don't want to be strong.
i just want to hear a heartbeat
that's been gone for too long.

find me there

sara rian

my life is now a string of deep inhales
getting me from one minute to the next.
frantically pulling air into my lungs
while my ribs and heart feel broken.
as though i am trying to make up for
the breaths you will never take.

find me there

sara rian

the worst part of a griever's day
is in the morning when they wake up and remember
that their person will never come home again.
and every hour after that.

find me there

sara rian

after tragic loss
you no longer
just wake up
from nightmares.
you wake up
to them.

find me there

sara rian

how do our hearts do it.
love someone so much
and lose them completely.
how do these little things
hold so much pain.
and love. and longing.
they should be bursting
from our chests and
dragging behind us
on leashes and wagons.
after all of the grief
one must live through
how do they still fit
behind our ribs.

find me there

sara rian

maybe i just keep moving.
i'll stay too busy to think.
too busy to remember grief.
i'll forget it ever happened.
i'll pretend you are waiting at home.
i'll hum in the car with my windows down.
no worries, just a few more things to do.
then i will be on my way back.
so much to tell you about my day.
see you soon, my love.
see you so soon.

find me there

sara rian

sleeping.
you're just sleeping.
your eyes will open
and you'll smile when
i reach for your hand.
for now you're resting.
you don't have to see
any more war or pain.
no cruelty or disease.
right now you're sleeping.
just sleeping for now.

find me there

sara rian

okay it's time to wake up.
you can come home now.
your cheeks are so cold.
my arms are so empty.
i miss you so much.
i've cried a million tears.
and questioned everything
i did and didn't do.
so this can be over now.
please just wake up.

find me there

sara rian

if the universe knew
how loved you would be
why did it not make
your heart out of diamond.
power it by the sun and moon.
and make it dance forever
with the oceans' waves.
if the universe knew
how missed you would be
how could it let you die.

find me there

sara rian

i don't know which
i'm more angry with.
death for taking you.
or life for letting you go
so easily.

find me there

sara rian

uprooted.
that's how to describe
losing a home that
took human form.
dangling midair.
wondering if you'll
ever settle in again.
knowing that even if you do
it will feel shallow and loose
compared to that place with them.
that place you felt you belonged.

find me there

sara rian

i thought it was okay to make mistakes.
i was convinced i could always try again.
that i could fix any problem handed to me.
until i couldn't make you breathe again.
until i couldn't will your heart to beat.
until i couldn't hold you without
ashes falling through my fingers.
and nothing could be undone.
now every day is a fight between
thinking i could have saved you
and feeling foolish for thinking
i ever had that much power.

find me there

sara rian

if you looked through the eyes
of the person i was
before they died
you would see
how blind i was.
to life's fragility
and death's appetite.
but look today.
through tears you'll see
fingerprints left on mirrors
in case one day
they're all i have left.

find me there

sara rian

how am i supposed to
rest and settle into life
knowing how things
are easily taken away.
how am i supposed to
truly feel happy again
while missing the things
that have been taken already.

find me there

sara rian

i will never take for granted
the warmth of a hand or
the pink of a cheek.
i have before and
never again.

find me there

sara rian

don't you grow up
we say to babies.
don't you get old
we say to adults.
but please do.
grow up. get old.
what a privilege.
what a gift.

find me there

sara rian

~~time is a thief.~~
time is a gift.
death is the thief.

find me there

sara rian

i don't want to smile
at the sun today.
i want to shake the sky
until it gives you back to me.

find me there

sara rian

death, why do you take the good ones.
the ones who bring such joy and love.
the ones who do good things. or could
if you just gave them a little more time.
the ones who have never caused harm.
i know you can't only take bad people.
but i see so many monsters around
with gray hair and wrinkled grins.
the cold hearts beating longer
than hearts made of gold.
death, why does it seem
like you always take
the good ones.

find me there

sara rian

because death is a bird
that will land on any tree.
an old tree. a sapling.
one still standing fighting disease.
one that just reached the canopy.
a tree with its branches
entangled with another.

death is just a bird.
that will land on any tree.

find me there

sara rian

i hate that people must meet you
through my tears and pain
when they should be meeting
you. just *you.*
they should see your smile
and hear your voice firsthand.
not through pictures or poetry.
i wish people could see that beauty
without the shadow of sadness
that now follows it around.

find me there

sara rian

half of my time
spent wondering
where you are now.
the other half
telling myself
it doesn't matter
if it's not with me.

find me there

sara rian

i have forever to mourn.
forever to grieve.
and on my dying day
i will still wake up
and look for you.
forever is not enough time
to accept that you are gone.

find me there

sara rian

if you were still alive
i'd be here talking
about love
and hope.
living life.
finding peace.
but you are gone.
and now the love
i talk about
is a lot less
hopeful.
and this life
a lot less
peaceful.

find me there

sara rian

the earth glowed so bright while you were here
i figured all the stars and planets could see.
but when your light went out
it's like the world only got
darker for me.

find me there

sara rian

i hate those moments.
when you are irritated in traffic or
you left dinner in the oven too long
and then you remember they're dead.
of course you never actually forgot.
your body just tried to feel normal
and get upset about the small things.
but now it freezes and it screams.
because you don't get to feel normal
when a stupid small thing happens
because it will always be
compared to losing them.

find me there

sara rian

how can you be everywhere
yet nowhere at all.
how are you still with me
but i'll never see you again.

find me there

sara rian

i see the ghost
of every version of you
that you didn't live long enough
to become.

find me there

sara rian

i could fill a library
with books about you.
paint murals across
every city in the world.
i'd write a thousand songs
about the magic that you carried.
you are worth every grand gesture.
but i miss our old. quiet. little life
when *i love you*'s could be whispers
because you were right here
to catch each and every one.

find me there

sara rian

i wish i had one more chance.
to stare at your smile longer.
slowly count your eyelashes.
hold your hand to my cheek.
i love you so much.
you knew that.
you had to know.
but what i would do
for one more chance
to remind you of it.
one more chance
to soak you in.

find me there

sara rian

there's no way
it could all fit
into an urn
or into a box.
could it?
all of that love.
their past.
their future.
every adored thing.
the galaxy itself
isn't big enough.
there's just no way
it could all fit.

find me there

sara rian

my grief. my longing.
it aches as the sun shines.
and it burns in the moonlight.
the days bleed into the nights.
no bounds. no edge. no rest.
missing you is ceaseless.

find me there

sara rian

so here we are.
another year without you.
they did say time would heal me.
it's becoming quite easy now.
like being held underwater
and learning how to breathe.

find me there

sara rian

how does grief
make five years
feel like five decades
and also five minutes.
like it has been ages
since i've seen you
but i still hurt as badly
as i did on the day
you died.

find me there

sara rian

i feel you drifting farther
as the days come and go.
i study my memories of you.
clutching onto every detail
because the years will pass by
and try to take you with them.
i know time heals some wounds
but it often rubs salt into grief.

find me there

sara rian

what happens
when i travel
down memory lane
and reach the end.
when i no longer
stumble across photos
forgotten in a box.
what will happen
when all of the stories
have been told.
and i have
nothing new
left of you.

find me there

sara rian

grief built a home in my heart.
right on the land
our new memories
were supposed to fill.

find me there

sara rian

i wonder if you are
wherever you are
counting the days
since you left here
like i still do.
i see my face wrinkling
in places you'll never see
and i cannot believe
you've been gone this long.
does your heart break today too?
or does it not matter how many times
the earth orbits the sun because
time cannot hurt you
wherever you are.

find me there

sara rian

the sun rises
and i'm reminded
that such beauty exists.
and of the devastating reality
that i'll live through thousands more
of these sunrises without you.

find me there

sara rian

i'll believe
that losing them
gets easier with time
when you convince me
that the earth is flat.
but until then
i'll wander the world
looking for their love
until i fall off the edge.

find me there

sara rian

this world is growing
all too comfortable
with your absence.
but not me. i won't.
keep me aching.
sore and tender.
tortured and
missing you
loudly.

find me there

sara rian

i will not
ask my grief
to be quiet.
i will not
let the world
shut it out.
i will not
watch you
die twice.

find me there

sara rian

you're my constant.
not just a moment
that came and went.
some trivial thing.
a flash of light.
my grief evolves
but missing you
and loving you
will pierce through
every layer left
of my forever.

find me there

sara rian

grief brings out
some of the softest
and ugliest parts
of a person.
and not just
the griever.
but of the people
watching them grieve.

find me there

sara rian

death already took my person.
so please don't take
my right to grieve
in this life i have left
without them.

find me there

sara rian

if it's okay for you to share
wedding portraits and family photos
and last night's dinner with friends
it should be okay that they share
a photo of their loved one.
yes. that one. over and over.
they only have so many.
maybe they only have one.
if it's okay to hear about your trip
then they can share their memories
or the dreams that also died that day.
if it's okay to share about life
it needs to be okay to share
our lives after loss.

find me there

sara rian

the energy it takes for
someone grieving to
wake. eat. or smile
could make the sun
look like a tiny spark.
yet we call them weak
when it goes on *too* long.

find me there

sara rian

grief grows on everything.
dates. things. feelings. memories.
like moss on once polished stones.
everywhere and won't be washed away.

find me there

sara rian

on an ordinary day
there is frustration. exhaustion. overwhelm.
we are allowed to feel without comparison.
but i hope we take time to remember
that when we curse our messy homes
there is a mother staring at a clean floor
begging to have her child back
when your parent calls you again and again
because the remote isn't working
there is someone listening to
their parent's last voicemail. again and again.
when your spouse comes home without the milk
there is a person in tears staring at a door
that their partner will never walk through again.
no. you don't need to wash away
the ordinary feelings on an ordinary day.
just make sure gratitude has a space to sit.

find me there

sara rian

if you're tired of hearing
about their person no longer living
imagine how tired they are
trying to live without their person
and making sure the world
doesn't forget they were here.

find me there

sara rian

a stranger's life may seem
like a tiny grain of sand
at the bottom of the sea.
but to someone else
that life was the
entire ocean.

be gentle with grief.

find me there

sara rian

they are in a better place.
maybe that's true.
but it isn't fair.
why couldn't this
have been the best.
right here. with us.
why does better
have to be so
far away.

find me there

sara rian

they wouldn't want to see you cry.
of course they wouldn't want it.
but they would understand it.
i wish you would too.

find me there

sara rian

you will heal.
you want to say it.
it feels like the right thing.
but you don't have to tell me
that the pain goes away.
that one day i'll be fine.
if there is anything
i've truly accepted
it is that i am okay
with not being okay
without them.

find me there

sara rian

don't be fooled.
they aren't better
or over their loss.
that smile you see would be bigger
if their person was still breathing.
those eyes would shine brighter.
that laugh would roar louder.
so please don't be fooled.
joy can return. but grief
will always be there
gripping its neck.

find me there

sara rian

if today
you didn't see their tears
it is because they hid them
behind the bathroom door.
or grief granted them numbness
while it napped in the other room.
perhaps they stayed so distracted
their heart forgot death took anything.
maybe their eyes simply could not keep up.
i do not know why tears didn't come today
but i promise you that pain did.

find me there

sara rian

you're right.
grievers do want attention.
attention on what they've lost.
how beautiful their person was.
how loved and cherished they are.
we talk and cry and share.
begging. wishing. pleading.
for you to notice
what is missing.

find me there

sara rian

a griever's imagination
grows stronger everyday.
we dream in the daytime.
we see their smiles and tired eyes in the morning.
we see them laughing in our quiet homes.
playing out moments with our person.
the moments taken when they died.
as if the years we played pretend as children
were actually there to prepare us for loss.
you will want to call us crazy.
but if you see a griever staring
into an empty room
just leave them be.
soon they will be back
and broken once more.

find me there

sara rian

listen closely.
grievers aren't only
speaking of death.
they are trying
to speak of
life.

find me there

sara rian

if you read the words
of a grieving heart
and they make you
look into your partner's eyes.
take your mother's hand.
hug your father's neck
kiss your baby's face.
if they remind you
to joke with a sibling.
to call your grandparent.
or cuddle your pet.
it won't take away
a grieving heart's pain.
but it can wake up love.
shake the cobwebs off empathy.
and wipe the dust from appreciation.
you won't undo their loss
but you can soften the world
they are learning to live in again.
and the world you'll be grieving in too.

find me there

sara rian

please don't be afraid
to sit with someone's grief.
it is just love learning to cry
and memories turning to gold.

find me there

sara rian

so many of us
walking around
with smiles.
holding keys
in our hands.
going to work.
having conversations.
shopping for groceries.
so many of us
coming home
at the end of the day
to rest our heads on pillows
and missing someone so much
that our tears bleed into our dreams.
and our dreams leak into our mornings.
and mornings start another day of grief
that we'll tuck inside our pockets
because the world just wants
to see our smiles.

find me there

sara rian

i am sorry
for the loss of your person.
and the million things that vanished
on the day their heart stopped beating.
and the billion things you must grieve
every single day that they aren't here.
and i am sorry that there isn't
a better word than just
sorry.

find me there

sara rian

when i call you *strong*
it has nothing to do with
holding back tears or
smiling while dying inside.
i mean you are strong
for holding their memory
and all of the love you shared
in those tired arms and broken heart.
carrying it with you day in day out.
making sure the world doesn't
move on without them.
i call you strong because
while every bit of you
is drowning in their death
you are holding their life
above water.

find me there

sara rian

these eyes weren't lucky enough
to meet the face you are missing.
but this heart has seen enough grief
to recognize it sitting in your chest.
it takes one look at your tears
and it sees that pain and love.
i wish i could've known them.
but through you
i will.

find me there

sara rian

we will sing them a song today
that they never got to hear.
we will show them a new sweater
that they will never get to see.
then on their smiling picture
a brand new kiss we will plant.
one that they will never feel.
and we grievers will do it again tomorrow
on a day that they will never touch.

find me there

sara rian

it shouldn't take bravery.
talking about your person.
talking about their life
and about their death.
it should be welcomed.
yet here we are.
in a place and time
where it takes bravery
to keep their memory alive.
griever, today you are brave.
but one day i hope that
you don't have to be.

find me there

sara rian

i see them.
the ones trying to rush
you through your grief.
the ones on the sidelines cheering
faster, faster. you're almost there.
little do they know
there is no finish line.
little do they know the reason
they can't look you in the face
is because you remind them that
life isn't fair and death isn't either.
you are proof that a person can walk around
with a gaping heart-sized hole in their chest.
your tears are evidence that nightmares are real
and sitting in that pain with you is too much.
they aren't cheering. they are begging.
faster, faster.

find me there

sara rian

they believe
the world just spins
and as time passes
our grief quiets down
and pain fades away.
but can't they hear it?
this world is a record
that never stops spinning
and it is always singing
our person's name.

find me there

sara rian

their death is your rebirth.
into a person whose grief could
move mountains and swallow oceans.
into someone who will cry more than the sky
and carry pain behind every smile mustered.
you may look the same as you did before
but the only thing that came with you
is the love.

find me there

sara rian

i know you say their name
and instead of that smile
a lump forms in your throat
and tears burn your eyes.
but say it anyway.
your heart will smile
even if your face
cannot right now.

find me there

sara rian

they died.
and you didn't do
anything wrong to deserve it.
when you tearfully whisper *why me?*
you are looking for the reason.
the reason you couldn't keep them.
wanting your agony to have purpose.
but this is not your punishment.
there is nothing to learn from this
besides how to breathe again.
how to inhale air and exhale their name.
we may never know why they're taken.
but we know why they were here.
to love and to be loved.
that is all the purpose
we need.

find me there

sara rian

your love is not measured
by how many breaths they took.
if they took any at all.
it does not matter
how long you had them.
a minute or a century.
love is not measured by time.
and your grief will not be either.

find me there

sara rian

how could they not be proud of you.
look at you loving them here.
carrying them like treasure
after their death broke
every bone in your body.
i know it won't feel like enough.
but right now they are somewhere
pointing at you with a smile saying
that's who i have waiting for me.
how lucky am i?

find me there

sara rian

they couldn't stay.
but their memory can.
don't let the world
forget their name.

find me there

sara rian

when we see a grieving heart
shattered into a million pieces
and we know we cannot
put it back together
or carry every piece
we can at least pick up a few
and hold them in our hands
with warmth and care.
this pain is not meant
to be held alone.
it takes a village
to grieve.

find me there

sara rian

normalizing death
is not meant to stop grief.
it is meant to carve space
into this cold avoidant world.
for grief to let down its hair
and take a hot bath.
to offer it tea and rest
instead of slamming doors
in its face.
talking about death
will teach arms
to cradle the agony
instead of pushing it away.

find me there

sara rian

there are no more
memories in the making.
so when you let me talk
about the ones i've lost
you are letting me
spend time with them
in the only way i can now.

find me there

sara rian

the stars saw me
crying again.
i always ask them
where you are.
they might know
but they cannot
tell me.
instead they stay
and quietly glow
until i fall asleep.

when someone
is grieving-
be like
the stars.

find me there

sara rian

it might not seem like much
when you talk about them
as though they are still here
or speak tenderly to my heart
knowing that it's living with
the reality that they are not.
but it means everything to me.
and there isn't a thing in the world
that i could do to thank you enough.

find me there

sara rian

i don't need to be
called pretty or smart.
my favorite compliment
will always be about them.
tell me how we looked alike.
how we laughed the same way.
that we could be so silly together.
tell me how proud they'd be of me.
how you can see their love in my eyes.
i will take any similarity. any connection.
any way to show me that while i exist here
they do too.

find me there

sara rian

i will let myself cry today.
for the ones who should be here.
and the ones who were ready to go.
for the ones who fill up my heart
but not their seat at the table.
for the ones in a memory
instead of a moment.
there is no joy in grief
but there is grief in joy.
so i will sit down and rest
after each spark of gratitude
and i will let myself cry today.

find me there

sara rian

some days
my grief
is a storm.
other days
it is sunlight.
we cannot ask
love and pain
to do the same
dance each day.

find me there

sara rian

the grief starts out so hungry.
waking me up all night.
keeping me in all day.
but i can't blame it
for its big appetite.
it entered the world
the day my person died
and all things are starving
when they are first born.
so i will listen and feed it often.
it will stay with me as it grows.
i know it will always be hungry
but maybe. just maybe
it will start to stay full
a little. bit. longer.

find me there

sara rian

the sadness and the guilt.
the panic and the anger.
feeling everything
and nothing at all.
when i don't know how
to be softer with my grief
i throw these things into a pot
and put it over dancing flames
and i let it boil down and down
until the only thing left to see
is the love that they grew from.

find me there

sara rian

my grief is now a part of me.
i will carry it until my end.
it is a limb. it is a heart.
but it can't be cut off.
and it can't be cut out.
so maybe my grief
is now more me
than any part
that came before.

find me there

sara rian

grief lives here.
it is no visitor to me.
you don't see it because
it is napping on the couch
after keeping me up all night.
it is running out to the store for soup
because it didn't let me eat yesterday.
it decided to take a day trip to the beach
because it too needs time to rest.
when you see eyes dry out
smiles curling or laughter
remember that grief
is not the visitor.
the other stuff snuck in
while grief took a break.

find me there

sara rian

you can't see them with me
but they are everywhere i go
and in everything i do.
the love.
  the ache.
    the grief.
i pour them into
my morning coffee
and i steep them in
my hot tea each night.
i lather them into my wet hair
and massage them into my skin.
they are tucked deep in my pocket.
they are hanging around my neck.
you'll never see me without them
and you'll never see them at all.

find me there

sara rian

imagine if you could see
all of the words
we whisper to the sky
hoping they reach
the ones who've died.
so much love and sorrow
would fill the air above
we'd forget that it was
blue.

find me there

sara rian

i am the promise
you whispered
as they closed their eyes.
i am the crowd
around their casket
saying sweet goodbyes.
i am the tears
you've cried each night
since they went away.
i am their name in the sand.
that picture in your hand.
i am the love that stays.

find me there

sara rian

this grief is a home.
it's a farmhouse in the country.
a witness to both birth and death.
it's a bungalow on a quiet beach.
salted from tears and the sea.
it's a loft apartment in a big city.
with exposed brick and wounds.
it's a little cottage by the lake.
a spot to sit and remember
their eyes and their hands.
this grief is a place
where all my loss
and all my love lives.
and it's their forever home.

find me there

sara rian

i have to remember
the beauty of the day
if i am going to survive
the sorrow of the sunset.

find me there

sara rian

their death
crushed me.
crumpled me up
like a piece of paper.
now as i bravely open.
as i slowly unfold and expand.
you will find love in every crease.

find me there

sara rian

just because you
could not stay
on earth and
in my arms
does not mean
you did not belong.
you still belong
right here.

find me there

sara rian

how badly i want to rush through this life to get back
to you. but you'd want me here. taking it all in.
devouring fresh air and sunshine. kissing faces and
hands. but do you miss me? do you need me there?
yes. but not yet. you want me here. to tell people about
our love. how sweet it was. how sweet it still is. i just
want to be with you. but i will hold on. onto life. onto
things i love. no matter how much your absence burns
my hands.

find me there

sara rian

i'd dig through every desert
and i'd drink every ocean dry.
i'd jump from every mountain
to search through every inch of sky.
i would do anything to find you.
i would do anything to see
that not even death
could take you
this far away
from me.

find me there

sara rian

sometimes i feel crazy when
the pain feels so overwhelming.
but then i remember the love
and it all makes sense.

find me there

sara rian

it isn't because we shared blood.
i ache and search for you because
the universe forged our two souls
from the same star in the sky.
and i won't feel whole
until i find you again.

find me there

sara rian

you are not a sweater
that gathers dust
in my closet.
or some passerby
i smile and wave to
when i go for a walk.
you are not an old story
printed on crumpled newspaper
being used to pack up someone's dishes.
i will not outgrow you.
i will not forget you.
i will not stop sharing you.

find me there

sara rian

i hurt
for all of us grieving you.
and for the ones who are not.
for either they did not get to meet you
or they do not know magic when they see it.

find me there

sara rian

i know you are dead
but did you really die?
you live in my every breath.
in every smile and every tear.
you dance with the moon
and shine with the sun.
you laugh in the wind
and sing with the rain.
i cannot hold you.
you cannot be seen.
oh yes, i know you are dead.
but you did not die to me.

find me there

sara rian

our minds could not foresee
how short our time would be
but perhaps our souls knew
the moment they met.
maybe that is why
we loved each other
like we did.
our souls knew
we'd say goodbye too soon
and there was no time
to waste.

find me there

sara rian

i cherished you then
and cherish you still.
a heart can stop
but my love
never will.

find me there

sara rian

thinking about your death
reminds me of how cruel
this life and world can be.
yet thinking of your existence
reminds me of the magic they can hold.
even if it isn't for nearly long enough.

find me there

sara rian

if someone misses
and grieves for me
the way i do for you
then i lived this life
exactly as i should.
not because i made
them hurt the way i hurt.
because i loved them
the way you loved me.

find me there

sara rian

i know how hard
it must've been
to leave us behind.
how badly you
wanted to stay.
but i hope you knew
you could never
truly leave us.
i hope you know
you stayed.

find me there

sara rian

i feel you.
on the days
when i laugh
and on the nights
when i cry.
that's the thing
about you.
you were there
for it all.
you still are.

find me there

sara rian

go ahead and ask me
if i would choose this life again
knowing i would be left with
only memories of you
and a lifetime of grief.
over
and over
and over again.

find me there

sara rian

i was put here
to love you.
not out of duty
but out of purpose.
now you aren't here
but my purpose
hasn't changed.
i am still here
to love you.

find me there

sara rian

you trusted me
to love you in life.
now you can trust me
to honor you in death.
i will not let you down.
i will not let you go.

find me there

sara rian

i write love poems to you
and whisper to the clouds.
i walk around barefoot
so you can feel the grass.
all this without even knowing
if there is anything after this life.
but i will keep doing these things.
i'm not missing any chance
to make you feel loved.

find me there

sara rian

this love is yours.
i can't give it to anyone else.
i love deeply. especially after losing you.
and i'll continue to cherish and adore
the people and things that deserve it.
but there is a spot in my heart
that holds love for only you.
your name is etched into it.
no one and nothing else
can have it.
so there it will sit.
and there it will stay.

find me there

sara rian

i shatter every day
knowing i won't see you.
and then every day my pieces
pull themselves back together
knowing i have another day
to tell the world about you.

find me there

sara rian

the guilt of not saving you
picks at my bones like a vulture.
but i will not let it take me away
from what matters most now.
honoring you with every bit
that is left of me.

find me there

sara rian

i've grown comfortable
with being quite ordinary.
i'm no expert in this life.
i haven't mastered a thing.
but i know for sure that
i'm damn good at loving you.
and i'll try until my last day
to be the best at honoring you.

find me there

sara rian

did you see
when i spoke your name and
other names echoed proudly behind it.
when someone looked at a photo through tears
and remembered how beautiful it is to love someone
as much as they do after seeing the way we loved.
when someone felt normal for holding an urn
and another bravely sang to a headstone.
can you see that although you are gone
you are still making this world
a softer place.

find me there

sara rian

i love the possibility of
your soul returning to earth.
that you could be reborn.
that we could cross paths.
you could already be here.
held in another's arms.
somewhere far away.
maybe too far for us
to love each other again.
oh i hope you feel warmth.
i hope you feel safe.
it may not be
my second chance
but i hope it's yours.

find me there

sara rian

i'm sorry i couldn't follow you there.
i could only walk you to the door.
it doesn't mean i didn't want to.
i just needed to stay.
so many of us
need to stay.
to teach. to love.
to honor. to wait.
your time was cut short
and there is work to be done.
it won't bring you back to me
but it will bring you to others
and you are too beautiful
to keep to myself.

find me there

sara rian

i look
and i look
but some days
i cannot find you anywhere.
and all i hope is that it is different there.
i hope you never have to search to find me.
please let me always be within your reach.
even if i cannot feel you there.

find me there

sara rian

when my tired heart
fulfills its final beat
and my hand slowly
pulls back the veil
i hope your face
is the first thing i see
so i can melt with relief.
because i stayed
and made you proud
and i'll never ache again.

find me there

sara rian

living the rest of my life
without you in it
will feel like eons.
but i hope for you
it feels like
only a moment
between you leaving here
and me meeting you there.
no waiting. no missing.
i hope as you turn away
from our last goodbye
you fall right into
our *hello again.*

find me there

sara rian

please remember me.
i will not look the same
as i did the last time you saw me.
if any of me from here comes at all.
but remember this soul that loves you.
for it will not have changed one bit.

find me there

sara rian

the part of you that loved me
will never wake again.
but the part of me
that loves you
never sleeps.
it never rests.
it dances.
it weeps.
it waits.

find me there

sara rian

these poems.
my messages in bottles
i send floating between worlds.
thinking maybe. just maybe.
they will make it to you.

find me there

sara rian

i have not healed.
or even finished surviving.
i am still no good at grieving
and i have not forgiven death.
i am no success story.
i just choose to talk about it.
the way loss tortures us.
the way it makes us scared.
and furious. and confused.
and guilty. so damn guilty.
but how it also makes us love.
how we push past death and time
and continue to adore them.
how we fight the shame and taboos
no matter how badly our knuckles bleed
because grief has been silenced too long.
you will still find me in the trenches.
i am the one holding out my hand.

about the author

SARA RIAN is a wife, mother, licensed therapist, small business owner, author, and poet. She began writing in 2018 and published her first book that same year. Sara uses poetry to amplify the voices of all grievers and shine light on grief's complexity. Among her published works are *Loving the Gone, We Are Carried, When Bones Bloom*, and children's book *My Momma Has a Momma Too*.

Made in the USA
Las Vegas, NV
10 September 2024

95082391R00079